Social Media Marketing
How to Master Engagement in 15 Minutes a Day

by Dwainia Grey

Copyright @ 2015-2016 Dwainia Grey

Permissions
Please feel free to take photos of this book (or your use of it) for the purposes of review or social media sharing. Please do not photograph the whole book.

Published by
GreyChild Communications
Toronto, ON

Social Media Marketing / Dwainia Grey
ISBN-13: 978-0994888839

ISBN-10: 099488883X

Table of Contents

This book is dedicated to my parents and my son that support me no matter what.

Chapter One
Clarity

Introduction

What is your ultimate goal for being on social media?

Many people are obsessed with the number of followers and likes they get on their posts. They forget about building traffic, finding new leads and getting sales.

In reality, likes and followers are a great way to track your progress but these numbers do not have much to do with the true metrics of being successful. Review engagement, the number of people who are commenting on and then sharing your posts which lead to increase traffic to your website, lead generation and eventually increased sales as your true form of success.

People think there is a bag of tricks to social media success but the reality is you need to spend time interacting with others, connecting with people and building relationships.

Participate in the conversation; make time to engage by commenting, liking and sharing others content. Start the conversation by posting valuable content to compel people to consistently engage with you and share your content.

Despite what the gurus want you to think there is no secret formula to social media success.

1. Create a strategy

2. Post awesome content
3. Daily engagement

The key to social media is being social.

In this book, you will learn about creating a successful social media strategy, what content to post to get engagement and how to limit your engagement to 15 minutes a day so you are not wasting time on social media.

15 Minutes a Day

The philosophy around "**Engagement in 15 Minutes a Day**" is to take time everyday to build relationships.

By planning and scheduling content on your social media platforms, it allows you to engage / interact with your community 15 minutes a day.

The biggest complaint I get is that people spend too much time on social media without seeing results.

So I answered the question how to maximize your online presence, reach and engagement while not wasting time on social media by creating this 15 minutes a day strategy.

The strategy is built for people that understand the value, impact and power of social media on their business and yet struggle to get clients online. This book is for you if you

- Want a clear, concise plan to get results
- Want to attract the right people
- Are ready to take action now

- Are ready to use social media to increase traffic, leads and sales

The fact is social media is about being social and by putting the effort in everyday you can make an impact on your success. Not only is being social important but people need to trust you and that is where posting valuable content comes into play. Preplanning content is efficient and less stressful. The right content can generate traffic to your website, and increase engagement. When you plan and track content, it's easy to analyze and learn how to duplicate success.

This book is based on the program I created "Awesome Nation Engagement":
- DE-mystify social media
- Develop your own strategy
- Create custom solutions to build your Awesome Nation
- Time-saving strategies and resources
- Get more visibility

The program also includes community, accountability and hand holding.

Engagement in 15 Minutes a Day is all about getting the exposure you need to build trust, and to getting people to know and like you so they will buy from you.

Why Social Media
Social Media is the New Word of Mouth

Unless you live under a rock, you should know that in today's world being on social media is detrimental to your success and a big part of online marketing.

In conjunction with having a social media presence, you need to have a website that serves as your home base where you should be leading everyone and capturing emails to build your list.

Social media is another online marketing tool; your website / blog is not only your hub for leads but also your hub for sales.

Social media is awesome for:
- Creating more exposure for you and your business.
- Promoting your brand.
- Growing your community
- Building credibility in your industry and become an expert in your field.
- Creating instant expert status; experts are sought after.
- Generating targeted leads 24/7
- Finding and engaging with prospects.
- Engaging with current customers, and providing customer service.
- Gaining loyal clients that will buy from you again and again.

Social Media Assessment

Where are your social media efforts today? Take this quick assessment and see what areas you need to improve on.

- ☐ What is the biggest challenge that you are facing right now with Social Media?
- ☐ What do you plan to accomplish?
- ☐ What have you done so far to get your Social Media campaign started?
- ☐ How much time do you currently spend on Social Media a week?
- ☐ Are you directing Social Media fans and followers to your email list?
- ☐ Are you currently using any of the following social media platforms?
    - ☐ Facebook
    - ☐ Twitter
    - ☐ LinkedIn
    - ☐ Google+
    - ☐ Pinterest
    - ☐ Instagram
    - ☐ YouTube
    - ☐ Other sites

Action:
Complete the social media assessment right now. When you complete the book, go back and review your answers.

List of Terms

Influencers – A person that has a large reach and/or impact through social media.

Keyword - Words people use to find you online

Keyword Rich – Using researched keywords to make you findable.

Chapter Two
Develop Your Brand Package

Branding

Branding is about the image of you and your business. The concept doesn't only include style, colour, and logos but also the image of perceived quality. It's about how you distinguish yourself from not only the competition but also everyone else. Branding builds trust, loyalty and motivates purchasing.

Social Media Branding works when you are authentic and transparent. Building a brand that represents you will enhance your confidence as an Empowerpreneur and it will do the same thing in the eyes of your target audience.

To create a cohesive brand:
- Be willing to share your story
- Show your personality and develop your voice
- Know who your preferred client (target audience) is; communicate the way they communicate to elicit a response
- Know what you offer; products and services you are promoting with every post.
- Research your competition to do better
- Be consistent with comprehensive style guide

Use social media to get people talking about your brand.

Your Story

A big part of being successful on social media is knowing who you are and letting others find out.

Know Your Why

What is the deeper meaning behind what you do?
I want to help _____ (your preferred client) get _____ (specific result) because it will help their life in what way _____ and this is important to me because _____ (how you want the world to change).

Use social media to get others behind your why.

Use social media to show why you are passionate about what you do.

If you have not done it already, define your business / personal values, mission, and vision. Building a solid brand has a lot to do with the mission and vision of your business. Your vision and mission are both a part of the branding process because they help define what your business is all about.

Action:
Write down your mission (or purpose) statement.

What is your vision? A concrete vision makes you think about the bigger picture and what you really want and it should help "pull" you forward so you can stop blindly charging into nowhere.

Remember to be open to flexibility in the path that gets you there and whatever vision you write down today WILL change... and that's OK.

Your Bio
- Why do you do what you do?
- How is your journey similar to your preferred client?
- What adversity have you overcome that that your preferred client can relate to?
- What's your manifesto?

Remember to establish credibility - What are some top results your clients have achieved?

Your Business
Give an overview of your business, how you got started, and what makes you thrive today. The overview should be positive and encouraging. It should also make potential clients think you are an excellent person to buy from.

Action:
Write down your story and a brief bio.

Your Voice

How will you use social media to show your personality?

Use your voice to tell your story and your message. Your voice is the way only you can express yourself and your unique view of the world. Your voice shows your style, passion, and beliefs.

Being authentic - true to you.

Action:
Describe your voice on social media.

Your Preferred Client

As part of your planning, you must know who you want to reach and why. Decide if social media strategy is to reach existing clients, new clients or both.

Find Out Where Are They Hanging Out?
- Facebook
- Twitter
- LinkedIn
- Google+
- Pinterest
- Instagram

Your Preferred Client is NOT the only person you will work with.

Your preferred client IS the only kind of person you will spend your marketing time, marketing energy, or marketing dollars attracting to your business.

If you market for every one, you market to no one.

Who is Your Preferred Client?
- The people you most want to work with.
- The people who want, need and are willing to pay for what your business provides.
- Where do you have contacts?
- Who would be the easiest clients to get?
- What group of people are you most comfortable with?
- Can you find them?

Research

The Internet makes it supremely easy to find data on just about any niche or segment of the population you can think of.

In addition to the web you can use:

- Surveys/Questionnaires/Polls
- Interviews
- Observation
- Focus Groups
- Industry/Association Reports
- Your Competitors
- Complete Market Research Worksheet
- Current Client Perception

You can't please everyone. Your goals, marketing, and energy all align to reach your preferred client. Understanding your preferred client brings clarity to your business and makes it easy to write content and marketing materials.

Know Your Client

Your audience is the targeted client base that you are hoping to reach out to for purchasing your products and services.

Demographics and Psychographics

- Gender
- Age
- Ethnic Group
- Relationship status
- Family
- Education level
- Work/Career
- Professional Experience
- Income/Discretionary Income/Earning Potential

- Talents
- Goals and Dreams
- Favourite Music, TV Shows, etc.
- Geographical Area
- Values important to them
- Characteristics
- Priorities
- Hobbies and interest
- Work ethic
- Personality traits

A big part of knowing where they hang out on social media is finding out who the influencers are.

- Who do they get information about their industry / niche from?
- What are they reading?
- What events do they attend?
- What groups are they a part of?
- What associations and organizations do they belong to?

By becoming a voice in the communities of influencers and groups and associations / organizations, you make it easy for yourself to be found and heard.

What Keeps Them Up At Night?

- How do they define success and failure?
- What's keeping them from their goals?
- What are perceived obstacles to their success?
- What are actual obstacles to their success?

Knowing and understanding your client allows you to provide better solutions as well as craft you marketing to the issues.

How Does Your Product / Service Solve The Problem?

What outcomes/return on investment do they expect from your services or products?

You need to learn what words or phrases the clients use to describe the problem and find solutions to the problem. Using these keywords in your social media marketing will help you be found.

Why might they not buy from you? Identify the most common objections/concerns your preferred client might have about investing in your services or products.

Learn about your preferred clients buying process. Do they research potential purchases online? (If so, where?) Do they make the buy decision alone? Who else might they need input or permission from to make a decision? Knowing where your client is in the buying process and how they decide to purchase is a plus when drafting your social media and website sales copy.

Your Preferred Client Avatar

You will have a solid understanding of who your target audience is and understand what their needs, interests, and goals are. You will understand how important your branding efforts are in influence of getting people to buy. Use the information above to create your Preferred Client Avatar. Give your Avatar a name and create all your social media marketing content directed to your Preferred Client Avatar.

Meet Linda, my Preferred Client Avatar. Linda is a 38-year-old petite blonde. She is married and a mother of two beautiful girls. Linda is a reiki master, nutritionist, and speaker on wellness. She is the buyer and manages the finances in the family. Linda wants to do less one-on-one consulting and move to online courses. To do this Linda wants a new website and a social media strategy. She is worried that by making this transition, her family will have less money. Linda is a perfect candidate for my Awesome Nation Allure program and the Awesome Nation Engagement Program. Linda can also become a consulting client. If Linda does not want to do it on her own she can choose my DFY – Done for You Services where we create her website and manage her social media.

Action:
Create your preferred client avatar.

Your Offer

How Does Your Product / Service Solve The Problem?

A big part of creating a brand for your business is proving to potential clients why your products and services are right for them.

Craft Your Message
WHO you work with (your preferred client)
WHAT you do for them (your gifts)
HOW you do it (your process / methodology)
WHY you want to share your message (your purpose)

What is your USP (Unique Selling Proposition)?

Plan out your product promotions for the year. Know what products and services to promote and when. By planning out your promotions, you are able to have your marketing collateral ready and create your social media collateral, blog posts and sales pages in advance.

The What - What products / services do you intend to promote on social media?

The How - Based on your story how do you deliver your gifts? Identify what you do with clients and how your preferred clients will digest the information. What is your process (system)?

The Why - Why do you want to share your message? According to Simon Sinek author of "*Start With Why*" and Seth Godin author of "*Tribes: We Need You To Lead Us*", it's a lot easier to get people to buy when they agree with your why.

5WH
When looking at your offer answer the 5WH
We already covered: Who, What, Why, and How
Where do you perform this service?
When can you do it and how long will it take?

When Crafting Your Message Distinguish Between The Benefits And The Features
Determine what the benefits are with the products you offer, the services you offer, and working with you personally.
Why does the customer benefit when they shop or buy from you?
You will have a very hard time establishing a brand if you cannot determine the benefits of your products or services. The benefits differentiate you to prospects and provide the emotional pull.

The features of your products and services are also important and they go hand in hand with the benefits. The features of a specific product should provide a benefit. Features are specific qualities that are built into a product or service; adjectives, or tangibles, of the product.

<u>Turn Your Features Into Benefits</u>

Feature	->	Benefit
(what the product/service IS)		(what the product/service DOES)
branded website		website that generates leads and sales

Your social media promotion should showcase a major benefit as well a compelling image and URL to sales page.

<u>Offer Must Haves</u>
- Benefits
- Bonuses
- Guarantees
- Testimonials
- Call to Action
- Connect & Communicate

Ensure Your Sales Page Answers The Most Important Questions
- What is this product/service?
- Why do I need it?
- When do I get results?
- How do I order the product/service?
- When does the product/service arrive?
- How much is it?
- What is included?
- Is there a guarantee or return policy?

- Why is this different from Joe Schmoe's product/service?
- Does it come in different colors?

Include Frequently Asked Questions on Your Sales Page

When a prospect is interested in what you offer as a product/service, she comes to the table with questions. With copy, you're not there to answer those questions so you have to anticipate what those questions might be to overcome potential objections in the copy. Those are the frequently asked questions or FAQs.

- Who?
- What?
- Why?
- When?
- Where?
- How?
- How much?
- Offer?
- Guarantee?
- Objections?

Take the time to craft your message for your business and individual products and services. Always lead prospects to your website either to capture the email and build your list or to an irresistible sales page.

Action:
Review your content for your products and services to ensure they are social media ready.

Eliminate Competition

Niching down is a way to eliminate competition. Your niche makes you stand out in the crowd. It makes you memorable. You attract people that want the solutions you offer.

Take the time to research competition. Learn what makes them different, and why clients should choose you.

Many businesses fail because they do not consider their competition. You need to do proper research about your competitors, learn what makes you different, why the customers should choose you, and much more.

What Makes You Different?

- What differentiates you from your competition?
- What value do you bring to your prospects?
- How does choosing you benefit your clients?
- Why do they like you?
- Why do they buy from you?
- How can you capitalize on your differentials in you social media?
- How are you similar?
- Do they have the same products and services as you?
- What types of online advertising do they use, are they successful?
- What is their campaign fails?

> **Action:**
> **List your top 3 competitors and do your research.**

Style Guide

Create a style guide to create consistency in your branding. A cohesive brand gives direction to both you and your clients.

Brand Values: What values guide your brand?

Brand Message: What is your brand message? Have all social media descriptions relay the same message.

Brand Image: Use the same professional quality profile and cover image on all social media platforms that represent your brand.

Tagline: What's your tagline?

Your social media style guide should address content and visual branding.

Voice: How will you let your personality shine? Will you show your sense of humour, your passions, and your interests? Are you fun, conservative or wild? List unique words, phrases, and spellings your company uses as well as tone. Write the way you speak – be conversational. Being professional doesn't mean boring or no personality. Being professional means providing valuable and easy to read content.

Buzzword / Slang: Are there buzzwords or slang that you use that will showcase your personality.

Quotes: What quote do you use in your business? What are your favourite quotes?

Spelling: Use consistent spellings, create a list of commonly confused words, and punctuation and grammar reminders. Limit the use of abbreviations and acronyms; if you do use them ensure that they are standard.

Hashtags: Create a list of popular hashtags for your niche. Use custom hashtags for your products, services and promotions.

Call to Action: For each social media post, you should have a call to action. What do you want people to do? Create some go-to call to actions you can use for example Download, Sign up, Join, Retweet, Like, Share, etc.

URL: Some people don't agree and prefer to use a watermark but I think having a URL on your image makes it easier for people to find and visit your website especially on Instagram where you can't click on links in posts.

Style: do's and don'ts

Style Guide for Visual

Logos: Logo use do's and don'ts, as well as logo variations.

Fonts: Define the font, size and style to use on your social media post images

Colors: Use your brand color scheme on your social media post images to be consistent.

Watermark: Define the font, colour, and images to use on your social media post images watermarks. It could be as simple as your logo or URL.

Mascot: Is there a certain mascot, cartoon you want to consistently use to represent your brand?

Stylized Images: Decide if you want to use separate images for blog posts, quotes, tips, products, etc. and how will they look; fonts, images, colors to use. Make your image attention grabbing, authentic and appealing. Also, review watermark, text overlay font, and text alignment.

Due to the fact that each social media platform has its own size and optimal size for their posts, it's a good idea to create a style guide for each platform. Optimal size for all platforms is 735 px by 1020 px.

Video: Create branded stills, covers, intros and outros, transitions and annotations for consistency and brand recognition.

Audio: Create branded intros and outros, music and transitions for consistency and brand recognition.

Along with your content calendar create a style guide for each promotion / campaign.

Have your style guide out when creating content for social media as a guideline and a reminder.

Using a style guide is a way to build brand recognition and brand awareness.

Action:
Create your style guide.
Download Image Cheat Sheet.

Reinforce Your Brand

Reinforcing your brand means that you back what you say you are going to do.

Chapter Three
Create Your Social Media Itinerary

Objective

What do you want from social media?

Before embarking on this journey, you need to decide what your overall social media objective is.

Tie in your social media objective with your existing business and marketing goals.

It's nice to get more likes and followers but using social media should lead to actual sales. Contrary to what the gurus say it is hard to see direct sales in massive amounts from social media especially when starting out. What social media does is provide an outlet for you to build a relationship with valid targeted leads that you can sell to.

Social media sales is secondary to:
- Building relationships
- Increasing reach
- Building your brand
- Engaging influencers, connectors and potentials clients
- Increasing customer loyalty and improving customer service
- Driving people to your website and events

Use social media as a tool to convert leads to sales and generate more leads and sales.

Many people wrongly only look at social media stats such as how many followers, how many likes, etc. Having 50,000 followers is no guarantee for sales. The real stats to watch is how many people are visiting your website, how many people sign up for your opt-in and how many people actually buy. There is a lot of time wasted on increasing followers, likes, etc. These are great indicators of engagement but not for your ROI (Return on investment).

Not only do you want to create an overall social media objective, create short-term and long-term goals to be able to measure success. Also, set realistic, achievable and measurable goals for each month. Monthly goals can be the of number of posts or number of new followers to engagement.

Also, know that with social media marketing you may not immediately see results or a direct return on your social media investment. It takes time and work to build an Awesome Nation™.

Social media is a race of endurance, not a sprint. No quick fix here. It's like being on a first date and the guy wants to take you home. You need to build the relationship first before you see any action.

Action:
Write down your main social media objective.
Write down at least 1 long term social media goal for the end of the year.
Write down your 3 short-term social media goals to strive for over the next 90 days.
At the beginning of each month write down a social media goal for that month.

Planning

Develop your social media marketing plan as an extension of existing business and marketing plans.

Which social platforms will you use? Which ones are pertinent to you business, and preferred client?
How many times a week will you post on social media?
What days and times will you post?

Do you want to assign posts to certain days a week? Throwback Thursday, Follow Friday, etc. or make up your own.

How far ahead do you want to plan content?

How often will you promote your own content (blog posts, events, products, and services) versus other people's content?

What type of content are you going to share? Review the "Content Ideas" section. What you share needs to bring value - always think "What's in it for me?" Try for a combination of educational, and engaging. You are aiming to get them interested in you, your brand, and your business.

Action:
Go through the list of questions in this section to start drafting your social media plan. When you finish reading this book come back and complete your social media plan.

Day-to-Day Management

Social media is not something you set and forget. Someone needs to maintain it and actively increase followers and engage.

As part of your planning strategy, you need to establish who will run the day-to-day management of your social media marketing.

- Who will create content? Images / Video / Copy
- Who will post content?
- Who will manage your social media campaigns?
- Who will track, monitor and report?

Resources
- Experienced Writer
- Professional Photos / Photo shoot
- Professional Videos / Video shoot
- Branded Graphics

Budget
- Start-up and launch budget
- Campaign budgets
- Ongoing management budget
- Advertising
- Design Tools (Canva, Pic Monkey, Hootsuite, Buffer, etc.)

Action:
Decide who will manage your social media marketing, what resources you will need and set a budget.

Social Media Policy

It's very important to set policies and guidelines for your social media marketing. As an Empowerpreneur, you may be the only one managing your social media marketing today but in the future as your business grows this is definitely one part of your business you can delegate.

Develop your Social Media Policy
What are the policies you will have for you Empowerpreneur business?
- Rules of engagement
- How to handle customer service
- What to say and what not to say
- Workflow / Schedule
- How to handle negative feedback /criticism
  - Clients, media or competitors
- Response time
- Crisis management

Action:
Create your social media policy.

Social Media Checklist
Branding

- ☐ I have a clear description of who my target audience is.
- ☐ I know what personality/brand message and image I want to communicate.
- ☐ I've created a username that will be easy to find, follow, and connect with.
- ☐ I have the same profile username across all social media platforms
- ☐ I consistently use my branding (image, logo, tagline, etc.) in all online communication.
- ☐ I use a branded social media cover / header images
- ☐ I've included contact information in my profiles including my URL.
- ☐ I have included a professional email address - @yourwebsite.com
- ☐ I have included my business location (where applicable - at least put country)
- ☐ I ensure I use the correct NAP - Name, Address and Phone number (where applicable)
- ☐ I've included a professional photo of myself.
- ☐ I have a complete about / bio section with links to website
- ☐ I have linked and verified my website (where applicable)
- ☐ I link to other social media profiles (where applicable)
- ☐ Each of my social media profiles is 100% complete

Planning

- ☐ I have a Social Media Marketing Plan that I use to help guide my online marketing.
- ☐ I have defined my social media marketing goals and know how I will track them.
- ☐ I've created systems to test and track my social media marketing goals and tactics.
- ☐ I've integrated my social media marketing tactics into my overall marketing strategies.
- ☐ I've used relevant dashboards and automation tools to optimize my time such as Hootsuite.
- ☐ I've documented the systems and tools I use so it can be easily delegated.
- ☐ I have created a posting schedule for the social media platforms I will be focusing on.

Content

- ☐ I've researched the best places to find content related to my topic and relevant to my target audience.
- ☐ I use the right tools to find, organize, and distribute content.
- ☐ I have developed a system to find valuable content to share.
- ☐ I make sure I share a good mix of content (Va Va VooM – Value, Voice, Visual, and Marketing)
- ☐ I'm creating specific promotions and offers for my social media audience - EXCLUSIVES.
- ☐ I use an editorial calendar to layout content for my blog, email newsletter and social media posts.

- ☐ I follow the top blogs in my industry to stay on top of trends.
- ☐ I create content to share on all platforms – Facebook, LinkedIn, Twitter, Google+, Pinterest, and Instagram
- ☐ I have at least 3 main #hashtags I use.
- ☐ I have made my website shareable with widgets and plugins
- ☐ I always check for grammar and spelling.

Engagement

- ☐ I've researched the social media platforms to use to reach my target audience.
- ☐ I have started to connect and follow people - co-workers, employees, past and current clients, people I admire, people in my industry, and my competitors
- ☐ I've invited my friends, associates, and clients to connect with me.
- ☐ I've joined the right groups, lists, and communities where my target audience hangout
- ☐ I participate in those groups by posting content, answering questions and starting the conversation.
- ☐ I comment on relevant blogs in my industry/niche.
- ☐ I respond to comments posted on my blog.
- ☐ I create and participate in contests, events, and special online activities.
- ☐ I spend 15 minutes a day on engagement – I interact with my Awesome Nation – answer comments (good or bad), respond to messages, share, retweet, repin, like and promote other people's content.

Action:
Review the social media checklist in this section.

Set The Mood

When planning, creating content, or curating content for you social media strategy set the mood.

1. Best time

The ideal time to create content is unique to you. When is your creativity flowing? Some people like to wake up an hour early, others prefer daytime and plenty prefer the evening hours. Know your optimal time to create posts.

2. Get Comfortable

Before you start, create the most comfortable and inspiring environment. What gets your juices pumping? How best do you work?

Noise Factor: Silence required, watching your favourite TV show, listening to music.

Place: Where do you feel most comfortable working from? Home, office, coffee shop, outside?

Sustenance: Have your favourite beverages and snacks at the ready. Is it a nice cup of tea, gallons of coffee? Healthy snacks or chocolate?

3. Playlist

If you like to listen to music, get your playlist ready. What songs inspire you? Or are you someone that likes to have the ocean or whales in the background? Or is silence golden?

4. Notes

Many times your best ideas come to you when you're not sitting in front of the computer. Get into the habit of carrying around a notebook or using a program like Evernote to jot down your ideas.

5. Schedule It In

Schedule weekly or daily time to write your content, time to find others peoples content to share (curate content) and time to publish content.

Action
Write down what your creativity atmosphere is: time, place, playlist or no noise, go to beverage and snack choices.
Decide what you will use for your idea keeper
Create your schedules
   Content creation
   Content curation
   Content publishing

Chapter Four
Prepare Your Content

Content Creation

What do I post?

People always ask what they should post on social media. The nitty gritty varies by audience (your preferred client), industry and you. What do you want to post about? The main objective of content marketing is using your message to connect with people.

The number one thing that all posts should be is valuable and useful or entertaining.

To increase engagement use headlines that catch people's attention, ask questions, ask for feedback and use call to actions in posts.

40+ Social Media Post Ideas

1. Valuable & Useful Information
2. Exclusive Promotions - Promotions to reward loyalty to fans
3. Contests - People really enjoy participating in contests especially if they are easy to enter & have great prizes
4. Host Live Events - Google+ Hangout, Facebook event or Twitter Chat

5. Testimonials - Screen capture testimonials from other social media, as well as case studies and client success stories
6. Call to Action
7. Blog Posts - Ensure every blog has a branded image
8. Events, Workshops & Seminars - Share online and offline events you are hosting or attending
9. Opt-in Offer - Free gift to build your mailing list
10. Photos - Pictures of you & your products
11. How to Tips and Guides
12. Business News - Updates about your business
13. Quotes - Motivation & Inspiration
14. Celebrate Holidays
15. Video - People love to watch videos
16. Questions / Poll - Ask community what they think
17. Promotions - Promote your products, services, sales and coupons, daily deals or loyalty programs
18. Interviews
19. Photo Caption - Get fans to come up with creative captions
20. Lists / Top 10
21. Celebrate Milestones / Anniversaries - 100 fans, # of comments, etc. Reward a fan for participation
22. Humour - People love to laugh

Images

23. Your Own Quotes
24. Events - Create a cover image and a sharable image for all your events
25. Step-by-Step Instructions - Offer download or video

26. Thursday Throwback - Can be of you or something that brings nostalgia
27. Question - Use a photo to ask a question
28. Selfies - Pics of yourself
29. This or that - Show 2 options and solicit feedback
30. Promotion - Every promotion must have an enticing image
31. Fan Quote - Take a screenshot of a fan quote
32. Product Shots - Pics of your products
33. Blog Posts – Create multiple image variations for each blog post.
34. Tip Sheet - Offer download or video
35. Affirmation - Positive affirmations
36. Customer Testimonial - Post a client testimonial or better yet post a screenshot of a client testimonial
37. Facts - People are fascinated with facts; post little-known facts related to what you do
38. Famous / Favourite Quote - Quotes are very shareable
39. Customer Photo of you product
40. How-to - Offer a download or video
41. Behind the scenes look
42. Infographic - Full of useful information

I have given you 42 post ideas. Think about what would resonate with your target audience.

Write down a few ideas you can start using today. Don't be afraid to try new things. Mix it up, see what works. Determine which posts have the most interaction and engagement as well as which posts drive the most traffic. Repeat and duplicate. Repost what works and if a certain type of post is always doing well create posts that are similar (duplicate).

You can follow the gurus and copy what other people post but it's important to note that what might work for others may not work for you. This whole book is based on my years of experience but each client is different and testing is a big part of creating a successful social media campaign. Every audience is different. It's important to track and monitor what is working and what is not working. Measuring which posts make an impact and then adjusting as needed is your key to a successful social media strategy.

> **Action:**
> **Write down 10 social media post ideas.**

52 Weeks of Content

Part of the 15 minutes a day strategy is preplanning. Develop a 52-week content strategy so you will have a post for every week of the year,

Create at least 52 posts based on the ideas given. It can be 52 quotes, 52 tips, 52 lists, 52 questions, or 52 infographics, etc. It can even be a combination of the above.
Batch out your 52 in one sitting or throughout the year and have it scheduled so you have a post ready for every week of the year.

With the 52 weeks of content think engagement. How can you get people to interact? What information or question can provide you with the most likes, shares, and comments?

Action:
Write down 52 ideas you can expand on later.
Download the 52 Ideas Brainstorming Sheet.

Content Curation

Every week you should be reading about not only your industry but also the interests of your preferred client.

If you are not keeping up to date, you are doing a disservice to your clients. You should be on top of the latest news and trends in your industry.

Take time each week, daily is best for research. Using tools like Feedly and bloglovin to gather blogs of interests is huge time saver.

Industry Influencers
- Start following your preferred clients interests and influencers as well as blogs your preferred client reads.
- Do a regular search for keywords and questions that they use to find you.
- Watch other businesses related to your business, and that are complimentary to your business.

Action:
List 10 influencers to add to your Feedly as well as follow on social media.

When looking for influencers to share their content you want real people that blog and real people that engage on social media.
Review how often they post, what they post about and what hashtags they use

1. Share their content
2. Engage with influencers
   - Share, like and comment
3. Comment on their blog posts

Look for awesome content everywhere on the web to share with your followers. Look for content in their other interests as well as your own. People who share great content, get as much credit as the originator and you become a source that people go to for information.

Be that source for your followers:
- Share news, events and articles of others.
- Support your clients by posting content that addresses their needs and issues
- Support your partners by promoting their content

Sharing others content allows you to collaborate and build relationships.

Not only are you curating content you are sharing content as well. Make your social media account the place for your target audience to check in on a regular basis to get updates and useful information. You want your followers to check your social media accounts even when they don't see a post in their feed.

Spend 30 minutes to an hour each week filling up your scheduler.
Use Feedly in conjunction with:

1. Platform specific scheduler (ex. Facebook Scheduler)
2. Tweetdeck
3. Hootsuite
4. BufferApp
5. Coschedule

Follow Influencers During Your 15 Minutes A Day Of Engagement

- Create a list.
- Add their blogs to your Feedly and share their content on a regular basis. Be sure it's useful to your audience.
- Add them to your favourites in Facebook, and private list in Twitter.
- Make a note of Hashtags they use.
- Engage on their social media - Share, comment, like, retweet, +1

Action:
Create a schedule for curating and scheduling your social media posts.

Campaign Manager

In addition, to regular social media updates and engagement, you might want to promote products, services, programs, promotion or a launch. These are campaigns that have a defined start and end date, they are targeted to reach specific goals and targets and are always measured for success. Other campaigns can include increasing followers or engagement, or reaching a new target audience.

I recommend running at least one promotion or campaign per quarter to reach your marketing and sales goals.

> **Action:**
> **Get the Social Media Workbook and Planner companion book that has a Campaign Manager Page that allows you to plan each campaign.**

Planning Your Campaign

When planning your campaign be clear about your objective and target audience. What social media platforms do you plan on using in your campaign? Know how you plan to track, implement and measure success.

Be clear about what product, service, opt-in, contest, giveaway or coupon you are promoting. Define a budget with outlined cost and expected return.

I always recommend a landing page, tracking link and hashtag for each campaign.

For every campaign have a compelling image, blog post announcement, and a follow-up blog post. When running campaigns on social media be sure to gather emails and have an autoresponder sequence set up.

If it's a contest or giveaway, include winner notification date and stick to it.

Does your campaign also include advertising?

> **Action:**
> **Get the Social Media Workbook and Planner companion book that has an Ad Planner Page that allows you to plan each campaign.**

For your ad, be clear about your objective and target audience. Which social media platform do you plan to advertise on?

Again include a landing page and tracking link specific to the ad. For every ad know before hand what is your budget and what you plan to spend per a day. Review your return, CTR (click thru rate), and CPC (Cost per Click) daily.

Campaign Success Tracker

- Did you meet your objective?
- What was your conversion rate?
- What worked?
- What didn't work?
- What was your audience response?
- What will you do differently next time?

Action:
Plan and implement a campaign for this quarter.

Va Va VooM™

When scheduling content, you always want to ensure that you are not always promoting, and screaming buy me.

Take the time to develop a healthy ratio of your own posts, others posts, personal posts, and promotional posts.

Most marketing gurus toot a ratio for content marketing. How many engagement posts to promotional posts. Or how many posts of 3rd party content, to your own content (1st party) to promotional. Ratios also vary by social media platform. I promote 4 aspects in my **Va Va VooM™** content marketing approach that adds visual to the list because a huge part of successful online campaigns is the eye-catching image or the must watch video. According to the stats, people are more likely to engage with images and stop to watch videos.

Value – 60% - Tips, tutorials, useful and helpful posts. On social media, you want to be able to not only showcase your own work but also work from others that your preferred client can benefit from your content and others.

Visual – 20% - Make use of images and videos - create branded images and video. Share visuals from those in your community and those that serve your Awesome Nation.

Voice – 10% - Show your personality - personal posts about you, showing your life, and a behind the scenes look.

Marketing – 10% - Promotional posts to sell and promote your products and services

---

Action:
Start monitoring your ratio and see what works best for you.

Image Cheat Sheet

You've heard the saying an image is worth a thousand words, on social media, image is gold. You will get more engagement by using an image in your social media post. When creating and posting images think of attention getting and compelling.

- What is the image for?
- Where will it be posted?
- What is the message / text in the image?
- When will it be posted?
- How many shares, clicks, and likes?

Image Size Requirements

Each social media platform has its own image size for profiles, headers / covers, and social media posts.

When setting up your social media profiles be sure to use the right size. Potential clients will judge you when they see too large, too small or unfocused images. Your social media account may be the first impression or even second impression and you want to ensure that you let people know you can get it right.

Action:
If you are not prepared to create a separate image for each social media platform create images at the optimal size 735 x 1020 or choose one social media platform image size to focus on.
Download Cheat Sheet

PLATFORM	IMAGE SIZE
Facebook Profile Photo	180 x 180
Facebook Cover Photo	851 x 315
Facebook Post Photo	504 width x any length
Facebook Tab Photos (Apps)	111 x 74
Facebook Group	801 x 250
Facebook Event	785 x 295
Twitter Profile	400 x 400
Twitter Header	1500 x 500
Twitter Background	1280 x 1024
Twitter Shared Image	440 x 220
Google+ Profile	250 x 250
Google+ Cover	1080 x 608
Google+ Post	497 x 373
Pinterest Profile	165 x 165
Pinterest Board Cover	222 x 150
Pinterest Pin	735 x any length
Instagram Profile	110 x 110
Instagram	640 x 640
LinkedIn Profile Photo	200 x 200
LinkedIn Background (Profile)	1400 x 425
LinkedIn Company Logo	100 x 60
LinkedIn Company Banner	646 x 220
YouTube Channel	2560 x 1440
YouTube Thumbnail	1280 x 720

Consistency & Frequency

In the last chapter, you established your goals for your social media. Keep those goals in mind. Especially when you're getting started it can be tough to get traffic and comments happening on your social media, but don't give up! Remember how your social media fits into the bigger picture of your mission.

And keep these two rules in mind:
1. Your social media is a work in progress. You can adapt as you go.

2. Never think of your social media as finished. Instead, think of it like a growing, developing part of your online marketing that can be modified and tweaked as you go.

Be flexible about your schedule, your types of posts, and adjust as you need to. This book is a guideline, a base for you to develop your own strategies. As you go along you will learn what your target audience responds to best and what works for you.

Be consistent: Don't post regular for one week and skip the next week. Keep top of mind by creating a schedule and being consistent. I recommend 15 minutes a day of engagement to promote consistency and to develop the habit.

Be frequent: Many people break up their 15 minutes in morning, afternoon and evening. They also decide how many times a week/day they will post by social media platform. You are not going to post as frequently on Facebook as you do on Twitter.

Be present: Respond promptly to comments and messages on social media. As part of your social media policy incorporate a response time. No matter what consider all interaction good or bad is an opportunity.

> **Action:**
> **Create your social media post schedule. How often do you plan to post on each social media platform a day?**

Editorial Calendar

Content is the key to success in social media. If you want to do well on social media (and online), you need to learn how to master content in addition to engagement.

One of the biggest challenges for most businesses with social media is consistently coming up with original content.

By creating a plan with an editorial calendar, you can have content ready in advance.

Create your content calendar with something simple like an online Google calendar, an Excel spreadsheet, a Word document, desk calendar or whatever you're comfortable with. Your content calendar should include your company's events, upcoming promotions / campaigns or products your company plans to launch this year. This is not set in stone, be flexible and ready to make changes.

Begin by blocking out the dates that you want to be sure you're sharing posts around a specific event or topic and then you can see what's left to fill in.

Next, review your promotions, campaigns, and launches. You may want to have posts ready to go for the whole week about your promotion.

Review your 52-week content strategy and start filling it in.

Next review your calendar and for each week decide:
- What type of content you will post?
- What days of the weeks you will post your messages?
- Will you use an image or video for visuals?
- Indicate which social media platform that you'll use with each blog post.

By planning ahead with dates you can refer back to, you will find your social media updates easier to manage.

Also, you want a way to keep track of posts to reuse them.

Action:
Create an editorial calendar for your social media posts.

Scheduling

For the "Social Media Engagement in 15 Minutes a Day" to work you must start scheduling content.

Create Social Media Posts in Batches and Schedule Your Posts

There is a big debate about scheduling being unethical and not authentic - As long as you are adding value does it matter when the tweet is published? Adding value and being truthful (not misleading) allows you to be more efficient. I draw the line at automating engagement. You should never send out auto messages on social media.

On a daily basis you should be sharing content with your followers:

1. Your blog posts
2. Original social media posts
3. Others content (see section on content curation)
4. Engagement posts (posts you see on social media that you share)

1-3, you can and will start batching and scheduling. Once a week, take time to create your blog posts and social media in one sitting based on your editorial calendar. Setting aside a block of time to knock out your content is the best way to stay consistent, inspired, and totally ahead of the game.

Batching allows you to focus on engagement during the week as well as saving yourself time, effort and energy that could be better spent on serving your clients.

Scheduling allows you to be strategic about the proportion of informational posts to promotional ones as well as how much and how often you promoting.

Prescheduling posts allows you to use the social media platform analytics / insights to find optimal time to post so you can:

- Publish posts at a time when the majority of your followers are online.
- Publish posts when you get the most engagement; when your posts are most often clicked and shared.
- Publish posts when you are available to respond to interactions

Prescheduling posts allow you to space out your social media posts as to not bombard followers.

Prescheduling promotions is a great way to run your promotions over a specific number of days without overwhelming followers.

Use scheduling tools such as Hootsuite and Buffer to pre-schedule posts and then spend 15 minutes a day on engagement.

With your editorial calendar, you can schedule as far out as you can for static stuff like holidays and annual promotions. I have already pre-scheduled my social media posts for Christmas.

It's great to have posts ready to go during the week but don't forget to monitor for timely news or trends. And promote anything new such as live events or speaking engagements.

One afternoon a week start scheduling your posts, add your promotions, blog posts, and any valuable information you curate to Buffer and Hootsuite. This is a great Sunday afternoon activity.

Action:
Create a schedule for batching and scheduling your social media posts.

Chapter Five
Bring Your Luggage and Connect with The Locals

Engagement in 15

Are you interacting with followers, potential followers, influencers, and clients?

Here are the 5 Steps to Social Media in Engagement 15 minutes a Day.

1. Set Boundaries

Decide on how much time you are willing to spend on social media. Consider how much time you have available and how important Social Media is to your overall marketing strategy. Facebook, Twitter, Pinterest, and Instagram are fun and can be a time drain if you don't set boundaries. You can spend hours watching video, laughing at memes and catching up with family and friends.

2. Schedule It

Use your editorial calendar and batching on a weekly, bi-weekly, or monthly basis to schedule social media.

How much time can you allot a month to pre-write and schedule posts?

How much time can you set aside each day for engagement - the time you spend to interact with people? For some, it can be an hour a day. I believe everyone can do social media in 15 minutes a day. You might be able to do it in even less. When in doubt, experiment and see what works for you.

Scheduling social media posts frees you up to spend more time serving clients. It also allows you to

- Increase Followers and Fans - (Expand Your Awesome Nation)
- Increase Engagement
- Stay Organized
- Reach your preferred clients when they are online
- Run promotions and campaigns efficiently over a few days or weeks

Using tools like Hootsuite, Buffer and others allow you to be active on Social Media but not sit at your computer all day or be glued to your mobile.

3. Do It

You have created your schedule now commit to it. Write and upload the posts you want to schedule. Use Va Va VooM - Value, Visual, Voice and Marketing when creating and scheduling content. You are not only scheduling your own content you want to incorporate valuable information by influencers and others that reach your preferred clients.

Schedule your curated content and become a trusted resource.

Only share valuable content
Share content that is useful to your fans and share content that expresses your personality

4. Use lists

Set up the lists in whatever way makes the most sense to you. Lists are a great way to distinguish family and friends from business, to divide business between vendors / suppliers and leads and clients and finally to segment leads and clients. Using lists to segment is a good way to build relationships with influencers as well. Set up lists on Twitter, Facebook and Google (Circles). Using lists comes in handy when building relationships as you can target a different person based on the list / segment you created to start a conversation.

5. 15 Minutes A Day Of Engagement
Remember that you always have the final say in how often and how closely you interact with people online. You can spend more or less time but aim for 15 minutes a day of engagement on all your social media platforms. You can spread out these 15 minutes during the day, some people will break it down to morning, afternoon and evening.

Analytics plays a big part in scheduling and engaging. Not only do you schedule your posts at the times when you get the most engagement, you try to be on social media for real-time interaction when you know your Awesome Nation is online. Check-in to social media various times a day to interact - and only when you have something of value you will do a live status update. Take this time to like, share, retweet, pin and respond to comments and messages.

Also, within your 15 minutes, reach out via private message to someone (the handy list) to make a new connection or build a relationship.

Make your 15 Minutes Count
- Share / Retweet / Repin
- Like (like posts of people in your network, influencers, and clients)
- Engage with influencers

Respond to Notifications
- Respond to any comments via private message, comments on posts
- Acknowledge any new followers, likes, and comments
- Thank and reply
- If someone is commenting on your posts, take the time to comment back.

The immediacy of social media can leave you feeling that you need to respond the moment someone sends you a message or comments on your post. Without boundaries, you can start to feel as though you have to interact 24/7 and this is where paralysis or over use of social media comes into play. You're always in control of how quickly you respond to people.

This is a part of your strategy, setting boundaries and doing what's right for you. Some will say it's good etiquette to reply as soon as possible, at least within 24 hours but the reality is there are no rules that say when you have to reply, does not even have to be the same day. With that said, note that Twitter is in real time and people have come to expect a timely response. If a prospect or disgruntled client is reaching out to you on Twitter, it is best to respond immediately because they will take a lack of response or "late" response as meaning you don't care.

Post a Status Update

Social Media is where you want people to know, like and trust you. Don't be afraid to showcase your personality and use your voice. Your followers / fans / friends want to know who YOU are - on social media, they want to connect with you as a person. By scheduling engagement, it may not be as authentic and real. Use this time to post about things that are important and from the heart. Personal posts build connections, so don't be shy.

Checklist

Depending on any campaigns or promotions my 15 minutes of engagement can turn into an hour of engagement but I ensure it's not wasted time by having a checklist that helps me be more efficient.
I look in my feed to find posts that are either beneficial to your Awesome Nation or stand out on a personal level.

1. Share / Retweet / Pin
2. Like (like posts of people in your network, influencers, and clients)
3. Comment / Reply
4. Respond to any communication via private message, or commenting on your posts.
5. Review posts in communities and groups to share, like, and comment on
6. Status updates if applicable

Once I cycle through my checklist throughout the day, sometimes when I have down time in the evening, I will use social media just for fun. I love finding things to pin on Pinterest, visit my little cousins Facebook page, creep (read posts without any interaction) my son's Twitter account.

Social Media is not just about strategically promoting your business it's a place where you can have fun too! Just don't get carried away where you don't know where the time went.

Action:
Create your 15 minutes a day strategy.

Facebook Strategy
If you're not on Facebook, you're missing out. Read Facebook Catastrophe on SlideShare.net.

Saying that you don't want to be on Facebook because of privacy issues is usually an excuse that you really don't want to be visible. Not using a real picture means you are not ready to take control of your business, your brand and YOU.

Facebook Strategy
- Is your preferred client using Facebook?
- What is your objective? How does Facebook tie in with your business goals?
- How is Facebook going to help you reach your goals?
- Why are Facebook fans good for your business?
- How can you lead a Facebook fan to buy?
- How can you add value to your preferred client life through a Facebook Page?
- How does Facebook tie into your content marketing strategy?
- How can Facebook help you capture leads to your email list?
- How can Facebook increase traffic to your website?

Facebook Branding
- Have you included a professional photo on your personal profile?
- Do you have a completed Facebook Page with a logo, and branded cover?
- Does your Facebook page about section include keywords and reflects your voice and brand? Does it include your website URL?
- Have you claimed your custom Facebook URL?

Facebook Content
- Post Regularly (max 2 times a day on your page)
- Post links, photos, events and video
- Post status updates to increase interaction: quotes, humorous, trending topics and breaking news, tips / how to's, and questions
- Share blog posts in status updates Facebook Groups, and Facebook Page
- Share other's content

Create a schedule (monthly / weekly / daily) for Facebook.
Use insights to help you create targeted posts and know the best day and time for engagement.

Facebook Engagement
Do have a (monthly / weekly/daily) Facebook engagement schedule?
- Post status updates and in groups
- Respond to all messages & comments on your page
- Tag people when you post their content
- Comment as your page

Make connections

- Influencers
- Current, Past & Future Clients
- Future Collaborators
- Family and Friends

Facebook Groups
- Utilize Facebook Groups to add value.
- Ask and respond to questions
- Post insightful comments
- Have a running list of what groups to join and/or start

Integrate Facebook on your website
- Facebook Profile buttons
- Facebook Widget
- Facebook Share buttons
- Embed Facebook posts on blog posts

Facebook Tools
- Video – Upload video direct to Facebook to get more exposure
- Photo – Create blog posts albums by category
- Apps / Tabs - Use Facebook Apps to add Pinterest, Twitter, Instagram, email subscription, etc., to your page.
- Advertising - Use Facebook Advertising to create super-targeted ads and reach your target audience.
- Get the Facebook Workbook and Planner

Action:
Create your Facebook strategy.

Twitter Strategy
Take your public relations to the next level 140 characters at a time.

Twitter Strategy
- Is your preferred client using Twitter?
- What is your objective? How does Twitter tie in with your business goals?
- How is Twitter going to help you reach your goals?
- Why are Twitter followers good for your business?
- How can you lead a Twitter follower to buy?
- How can you add value to your preferred clients life through Twitter?
- How does Twitter tie into your content marketing strategy?
- How can Twitter help you capture leads to your email list
- How can Twitter increase traffic to your website?
- How can Twitter connect you locally?

Twitter Branding
After creating your strategic Twitter plan, the first thing you want to do is ensure you have a winning profile. Be sure to create a good biography with a current professional photo for your Twitter profile. Most people won't follow a company with no photo because they can't put a name to the company and don't feel a connection to them. – If your brand is you, upload a nice, friendly photograph of yourself. Otherwise, you could make it your business logo. Brand your profile with an awesome header image. Don't be afraid to add your location to attract local clients and use #hashtags to attract your preferred client. And most important add a link to your website.

Just like with all online marketing keywords are important.

Link to other social media profiles

Hashtags
Always use **#hashtags** to make your tweets findable. Use hashtags in your tweets to get more eyes on you, get more interest and more followers.
The number sign (#) followed by a keyword will categorize your Tweet so that others can easily find it. Using hashtags will also get you picked up in Daily News .ly papers. These are great little places to get noticed by more readers.

Make a list of hashtags to use:
- That your preferred client uses.
- For your industry and niche
- Influencers are using
- Custom hashtags for your products, services, and promotions
- Trending hashtags

Twitter Content
- Post links, photos, and video
- Share Blog Posts
- Share other's content
- Post Regularly
- Preface posts with comments
- Post status updates to increase interaction: quotes, humorous, trending topics and breaking news, tips / how to's, questions and meaningful insights.

Create a tweet schedule for Twitter

Use Twitter Analytics to create targeted posts

Twitter Engagement

- Post updates
- Retweet
- Respond
- Favourite
- Mention
- Direct Message

Do you have a Twitter engagement schedule?

<u>Make Connections and Follow</u>

- Influencers
- Current, Past & Future Clients
- Future Collaborators
- Family and Friends

Periodically clean up your Twitter feed and unfollow spam and inactive accounts.

Use **Twitter Lists** to manage your feed.
Create lists for current and past clients, influencers, future clients, etc. Using lists makes it easy to interact and helps with 15 minutes a day engagement.

Twitter Chats

A Twitter chat is where a group of users meet on Twitter at a scheduled time using a designated hashtag (#) to discuss a certain topic for about an hour (1 hour max). The host will post questions using Q1, Q2... to get participants to answering normally using A1, A2.

Use Twitter Chats to add value
- Ask and respond to questions

- Post insightful comments
- Participate in niche, industry, and interests chats
- Have a running list of what chats to join and/or start

Don't start hosting your own chat until you have experience attending a chat. Choose a concise hashtag that relays what the chat is about, and consider keywords and branding. Have your questions ready ahead of time and use special guests. Choose a time that your audience is online and does not conflict with the popular chats. Promote your chat in the days and hours leading to it on Twitter as well as other social media platforms; register your chat on Twubs. During chat keep it exciting and engaging - ask and answer questions, share resources, manage the conversation.

Integrate Twitter on your website
- Twitter Profile buttons
- Twitter Widget
- Twitter Share buttons
- Embed Twitter posts on blog posts and/or testimonials
- Use click to Tweet

Twitter Tools
- Lists – Create public and private lists
- Images & Video – Post branded photos and videos
- Twitter Cards – Add twitter cards to your website
- Use Twitter Ads
- To find Twitter Chats: Chat Salad, http://tweetreports.com/twitter-chat-schedule/, http://twubs.com/twitter-chats
- Manage Twitter Chats: TweetChat, Hootsuite, TweetDeck, Use Storify to create Twitter Chat Summary

- Get the Twitter Workbook and Planner

Action:
Create your Twitter strategy.

LinkedIn Strategy

Use LinkedIn to connect with business partners and clients, recruit, ask for advice and showcase your expertise.

LinkedIn Strategy

- Is your preferred client using LinkedIn?
- What is your objective? How does LinkedIn tie in with your business goals?
- How is LinkedIn going to help you reach your goals?
- Why are LinkedIn connections good for your business?
- How can you lead a LinkedIn connection to buy from you?
- How can you add value to your preferred clients life through LinkedIn?
- How does LinkedIn tie into your content marketing strategy?
- How can LinkedIn help you capture leads to your email list?
- How can LinkedIn increase traffic to your website?
- How can LinkedIn connect you locally?

LinkedIn Branding

After creating your strategic LinkedIn plan, the first thing you want to do is ensure you have a winning profile. Optimize your profile so it is 100% complete. Just like with all online marketing keywords are important but don't keyword stuff. Include your keywords on your Headline, Work Experience, Summary and Specialties. Don't forget about Interests, Groups & Associations, Honours & Awards; be more visible so more people can connect with you, the more likely they will want to do business with you.

Your LinkedIn profile is a reflection of your professional image, so ensure your profile is correctly formatted and free of spelling and grammatical errors. Include a professional photo, with your branded bio – stick to your brand message.

Complete your LinkedIn Company Page and Showcase Pages to promote your products and services.

LinkedIn Content
Utilize LinkedIn Posts with compelling content and images
Share your blog posts in Groups, Status Updates, and Company Page
Share other's content
Links
Post Regularly

Create a LinkedIn content schedule.

LinkedIn Engagement
- Post status updates at least once a week
- Engage in groups
- On a regular basis endorse and recommend others

Continually Make New Connections - Think of the potential to reach your connections, connections - how big is their LinkedIn network?

- Influencers
- Current and Past Clients
- Future Clients
- Future Collaborators
- Family and Friends

Become a connector. Use LinkedIn to make introductions and referrals.

Do you have a LinkedIn engagement schedule?

LinkedIn Groups
- Use LinkedIn Groups to add value
- Ask and respond to questions
- Post insightful comments
- Have a running list of LinkedIn groups to join and/or start

LinkedIn Tools
- Projects – projects you have worked on and completed
- Publications – books, eBooks, workbooks, planners, etc. you have created
- Portfolio – showcase your work / creations
- Get the LinkedIn Workbook and Planner

Action:
Create your LinkedIn strategy.

Google+ Strategy

Build credibility with Google+. Google+ plays a big part in SEO, branding and your authority on Google.

Google+ Strategy

- Is your preferred client using Google+?
- What is your objective? How does Google+ tie in with your business goals?
- How is Google+ going to help you reach your goals?
- Why is a Google+ account good for your business?
- How can you lead a Google+ friend to buy?
- How can you add value to your preferred clients life through a Google+ page?
- How does Google+ tie into your content marketing strategy?
- How can Google+ help you capture leads to your email list?
- How can Google+ increase traffic to your website?
- How can Google+ connect you locally?

Google+ Branding

Create a Google+ profile page and include a professional photo.

Create a branded Google+ Business Page with keyword rich description, tagline, and URL. Strengthen your brand recognition by having your company logo, and a branded cover image. Post your branded, photos, and videos (link your YouTube account) on your page. Also, ensure your contact information is correct and include links to your website and other social media profiles. Your Google+ Page is integrated with Google Maps to help visitors find you if you have a physical location it's great for local SEO and draws in locals.

Claim Google+ authorship and your custom URL.

Google+ Content
- Post texts, links, photos, events, and video to your profile and Google+ Page.
- Share Blog Posts in Communities, Status Updates, and Google+ Page
- Share other's content
- Always use #hashtags.
- Use keywords and descriptions
- Be consistent
- Vary posts - long and short
- Schedule posts
- Post Regularly

Create a schedule for Google+.
Use Google Analytics to create targeted posts.

Google+ Engagement
- Share, +1, and comment others posts.
- Mention others ("+" in front of name) when you share their content and respond to mentions.
- Thank people who share your content
- Share Google+ posts on other social media profiles
- Follow back those that circle you
- Reply to comments

Make new connections by continually adding to your circles.
- Influencers
- Current, Past & Future Clients
- Future Collaborators
- Family and Friends

Do you have a Google+ engagement schedule?

Google+ Communities
Use Google+ Communities to add value
Ask and respond to questions
Post insightful comments at least once a week
Have a running list of what groups to join and/or start

Integrate Google+ on your website
- Google+ Badge
- Google+ Profile buttons
- Google+ Share buttons

Google+ Tools
- Create Targeted Circles – Influencers, clients, prospects and top engagers
- Google+ Communities – Join communities and follow members
- Attend and Host Google+ Hangouts – Live on air, webinar, panel discussion, video conference, video call, client meetings, screen share, etc.
- Google Reviews - Get reviews, the majority of people that search for local businesses online take action by visiting or contacting the business and they also trust online reviews.
- Get the Google+ Workbook and Planner

Action:
Create your Google+ strategy.

Pinterest Strategy

The majority of Pinterest users are women who love pins on recipes, DIY (Do It Yourself) and Fashion. How can your Pinterest posts appeal to them?

Pinterest Strategy

- Is your preferred client using Pinterest?
- What is your objective? How does Pinterest tie in with your business goals?
- How is Pinterest going to help you reach your goals?
- Why are Pinterest followers good for your business?
- How can you lead a Pinterest follower to buy?
- How can you add value to your prospect's life through Pinterest?
- How does Pinterest tie into your content marketing strategy?
- How can Pinterest help you capture leads to your email list?
- How can Pinterest increase traffic to your website?

Pinterest Branding

After creating your strategic Pinterest plan, the first thing you want to do is ensure you have a branded keyword rich profile with a professional photo or logo. You also want to get verified with a business account and claim your custom Pinterest URL. Lastly, create unified branded Pinterest board covers.

Pinterest Content

- Share Blog Posts on multiple boards. Ensure each blog post has a pinnable image and make more than one image per blog posts. When posting images to your blog create your keyword rich pin description in your alt tags.

- Share other's content
- Post Regularly
- Schedule posts
- Use #hashtags
- Vary vertical and horizontal images

Create a schedule for Pinterest.
Use Pinterest Analytics to see what images people are pinning and to create more pinnable images.

Pinterest Engagement
- Follow users
- Repin, like and comment on others posts.
- Respond to mentions
- Tag others

Consistently follow others
- Influencers
- Current, Past & Future Clients
- Future Collaborators
- Family and Friends

Do you have a Pinterest engagement schedule?

Pinterest Group Board
- Use Pinterest Group Boards to add value and increase your reach.
- Post insightful comments
- Have a running list of group boards to join and to start

Integrate Pinterest on your website
- Pinterest Profile buttons
- PinIt button
- Pinterest Widget
- Pinterest Share buttons
- Embed Pinterest boards and posts on blog posts

Pinterest Tools
- Boards – Organize and SEO your boards with optimized board names and descriptions
- Video – Pin branded videos
- Use Pinterest Advertising
- Get the Pinterest Workbook and Planner

Action:
Create your Pinterest strategy.

Instagram Strategy
Be personable, real and authentic.

Instagram Strategy
- Is your preferred client using Instagram?
- What is your objective? How does Instagram tie in with your business goal?
- How is Instagram going to help you reach your goals?
- Why are Instagram followers good for your business?
- How can you lead an Instagram follower to buy?
- How can you add value to your prospect's life through Instagram?
- How does Instagram tie into your content marketing strategy?

- How can Instagram help you capture leads to your email list?
- How can Instagram increase traffic to your website?

Instagram Branding
Develop a keyword rich bio with professional photo or logo on your profile.
Also, include your contact information and URL to your website.

Develop an overall theme to your posts, with a nice color scheme.

Instagram Content
- Use short, keyword rich descriptions on posts
- Post quality images and video
- Share Blog Posts
- Share other's content
- Post Regularly (add at least one new image daily - 2x max)

Share Instagram posts on other social media

Hashtags
Use hashtags to get found on Instagram. Posts with hashtags get more interaction than posts without. Ensure you add relevant #hashtags to posts. Hashtags are a great way to organize and categorize your posts making your images searchable.
Use #hashtags in comments
Use custom #hashtags on promotions, products, and services, etc.
Don't spam hashtags, users will ignore your posts and even blacklist your business if you routinely abuse and

spam hashtags. Relevancy is important when using hashtags.

Create a List of Hashtags
- That your preferred client uses.
- For your industry and niche
- Influencers are using
- Hashtags that get you the most interactions

Create a content schedule for Instagram.

Instagram Engagement
- Like, and comment other people's content
- Tag people when you use their products and services in your image. Unless it's a brand only tag people you know.
- Follow and follow back
- Respond to comments

Consistently Expand Your Network And Follow
- Influencers, bloggers, and brands
- Current, Past & Future Clients
- Future Collaborators
- Family and Friends

Do you have an Instagram engagement schedule?

Integrate Instagram on your website
- Instagram Profile buttons
- Instagram Widget
- Embed Instagram posts on blog posts where applicable

Instagram Tools

- Filters – Visual effects over images and videos
- Video – Upload 3-15 second video directly to Instagram
- Get the Instagram Workbook and Planner

Action:
Create your Instagram strategy.
What are the 3 most used hashtags for your niche / industry?

YouTube Strategy
4 Biggest Reasons to Start Using Video Today

1. Videos are an effective branding strategy allowing you to build brand awareness, promote and control your brand.
2. Great for search engine optimization (SEO)
3. Increase in click thru rates, leads, and sales
4. Easy to monitor and track

YouTube Strategy

- What do you want to achieve with each video? Have a clear call to action in each video.
- How can you add value to your prospect's life through a video?
- How does video tie into your content marketing strategy?
- How can video help you capture leads to your email list?
- How can video increase traffic to your website/blog?
- How can video help you gain a new client?

YouTube Branding

- You included a professional photo on your personal profile.
- You have a completed YouTube Channel (Icon, Art, Description, Links and URL)?
- Create branded preview image
- You have created a branded video intro and outro
- Optimize your Video (Keyword in Title, Description and Tags)
- Use playlists
- Use YouTube Analytics to create targeted videos
- Use annotations - text, links, and graphics placed over video
- Link to other social media platforms

YouTube Content

Create a video editorial calendar and schedule for YouTube

Use SEO when you create the video title, description, and tags.

Vary content:

- Website welcome messages
- Commercials for your products and services (average commercial 90 seconds)
- Reviews, demos, and tutorials of your products and products you use
- Contests
- Client Testimonials
- Tips and Tutorials
- Screencasts
- Webinars
- Behind the scenes look

- Your speaking at events

People are bombarded with "look at me" online. You want to be able to grab their attention and hold their attention. Create quality videos with good lighting and sound, and use bells and whistles to make your videos pop such as music, graphics, and bright colours. When it comes to online viewers, they have short attention spans.

YouTube Engagement
- Share videos on other social media channels
- Subscribe to others YouTube Channels. Like, share and comment on their videos.
- Respond to comments

Connect And Engage With
- Influencers
- Current, Past & Future Clients
- Future Collaborators

Create a YouTube engagement schedule.

Integrate YouTube on your website
- YouTube Profile buttons
- YouTube Widget
- YouTube Share buttons
- Embed YouTube posts on blog posts

YouTube Tools
- Playlists – Group services, tutorials, client resources, or theme categories
- G+ Hangouts – Create live broadcasts on YouTube

> **Action:**
> **Create your youtube strategy.**
> **List channels to subscribe / start**
> **List playlists to start.**

Call to Action

A lot of designers / creatives will make a marketing piece real pretty but the miss the mark by not asking for the sale. All marketing collateral should have a call to action. Even your business card. What do you want people to do? Tell them!

Not using a call to action on your social media posts is a missed opportunity.

What do you want your followers to do? Call, Email, Download or Purchase? Tell followers what you want them to do. With each post add a call to action. Click here, like, comment, share, etc.

It can be subtle such as adding your URL to every image.

Based on your monthly goals develop a call to action for each campaign, and for each post. Use your images to relay benefits - Focus on the outcome, people want to know how your offer will change their lives, not the product features.

Communicate urgency in your promotional posts - Most people react out of fear of missing out
- Now
- Today
- Act now
- Limited time only

- Limited quantity
- Enter soon
- On sale
- This week only
- Don' miss out
- Etc.

Action:
Create a list of Call To Actions you plan to use in your
social media marketing.

Communities
Using Groups and Communities
One of the key things in building relationships on social
media are groups and communities on the social media
platforms you use. Remember: people do business with
other people that they know, like and trust. That means
you'll usually need to build a relationship with someone
before they're willing to work with you or invest in your
offerings. DO NOT join groups to just to sell and push
your offerings. Support, encourage and provide value to
other community members.

Join The Discussion.
Always read the group / community guidelines. Most
have guidelines around what is and isn't acceptable when
it comes to promoting yourself or something you offer.
Find out what these are and respect them! Also, many
communities have specific threads devoted to promotion,
or specific days where you can self-promote. Even if they
don't, however, most community moderators don't object
to you mentioning a product or service if it's directly
relevant to something another community member asked
about.

If in doubt, ask the administrator of the group.

1. When you join introduce yourself to the group and let them know why you are there.

2. Respond to as many questions and comments from other people as you helpfully can. Establish yourself as a trustworthy source. Become top of mind when people think of the services / products you provide when they need it or know someone that does.

3. Start discussions with open questions. Avoid yes or no answers - and get people engaged by asking "How" and "Why". Keep the conversation going by moderating and participating in the comments.

4. Look for ways to naturally promote your offers. If you see a post where your products / services can add value let them know in a non-obtrusive way. For example someone asks for feedback on their new website, you would respond with "As a web designer you think..."
A question may relate directly to one of your free gifts or blog post, you would post a link to it saying, "Read this it might help". Sometimes it may not even be your blog post but someone else's blog post, you will post a link to it because you always want to add value to the group.
Or if someone is asking specifically for help respond in the post and take it to private message to get the details.
For Example "you need a web designer" you will respond with "you design web sites - you will PM for more details" (PM = Private Message)

5. Promote their offer to your Awesome Nation. If you see something that is relevant and beneficial to your Awesome Nation, share it with your Awesome Nation in the groups and pages you own.

6. Start your own group!

7. Promote yourself! Ensure the group allows self-promotion - please don't try it if guidelines outright prohibit it! - You will get banned from the group and possibly labeled a spammer. It's best to start promoting after you've already established yourself as someone who's known, liked and trusted.

Action:
Go through each social media platform you are active on and
   1. Join 5 groups
   2. Brainstorm a group you can start if you don't have one already.

New to Social Media

The best way to figure out which social media platform is best for you is to know where your preferred client hangs out and which one you are most comfortable with. Try out each social media platform for 10 days.

1. Set up your profile
2. Create a strategy for that week
3. Spend a week implementing the strategy

This is just an experiment for you to get comfortable with the social media platform this is not meant to generate leads or sales. Do the 10-Day Challenge:

Day 1 - Set Up Profile
Day 2 - Set Up Scheduling
Day 3 - Invite Others
Day 4 - Start Engaging

Day 5 - Share Content
Day 6 - Find and connect with Influencers
Day 7 - Write a status update
Day 8 - Spend an hour looking around at the various tools and privacy settings
Day 9 - Evaluate - Is This a Tool You Can Dedicate 5 minutes a day to?
Day 10 - Start Promoting the fact you are on that social media channel

After trying out the different social media platforms you may find that none really float your boat so, I recommend hiring someone to manage if for you or choose ONE social media channel as your prime hangout. Always keep your other social media accounts for branding purposes and choose two that you will visit on occasion. But the ONE social media platform you do choose make sure that you are a 100% committed and master it.

Action:
Take the social media platforms for a test drive.

Chapter Six
Stay Connected

Website Integration

The ultimate call to action of your social media accounts is to drive people to your website. Your website headquarters is the home of your own content, your awesome opt-in offer, and your sales pages.

You do want to let people know about your social media platforms by showcasing your social media profile links on one or all of these areas of your website:

- Contact Page
- About Page
- Sidebar
- Footer

Include a social media widget - Choose a Social Media Platform that you are most active on - does it fit your design?

In addition, add social media share buttons to your website to motivate sharing.

Encourage Engagement on Your Website With Comments

Enable commenting on your blog posts
Check daily and respond to any comments

Action:
Integrate your social media into your website.

SEO

All online marketing is SEO (Search Engine Optimization)

To be found online you must use the terms people are searching for to optimize your social media profiles.

With social media marketing, you need to get really clear on who you are, who your preferred client is and the results you provide.

At the core of all social media sites are search engines:
- LinkedIn relies heavily on your job title and description
- Twitter: hashtags
- Facebook: edgerank
- Instagram: hashtags
- Pinterest: boards
- Google+: it's Google

Use Search Engine Optimization (SEO) in Your Social Media Strategy

1. Do your keyword research. What terms are people using to find you? Pay attention to your Google analytics organic search terms.
2. Optimize your profiles for SEO. Have at least one constant keyword in all your descriptions.
3. Constantly use keyword rich hashtags.
4. Name images using keywords.
5. Watch industry trends and be ready to weigh in your opinion with blog posts and social media updates.
6. Monitor Google trends and Twitter trends. Join the conversation with status updates, and comments integrated with hashtags when relevant.

7. Post all your blog posts to social media. Even if you only use one social media platform as your main account. Take time to schedule your posts to other social media platforms to get backlinks and build social currency and clout.

8. In addition to posting your blog posts on social media platforms use social bookmarking sites such as Delicous, StumbleUpon, Digg and Reddit. Slowly bookmark all pages of your website not just blog posts to these sites. Just like with any other social media share others content too.

9. Always post your blogs to your Google+ page.

10. In addition to sharing your blog posts, start guest blogging and commenting on others blogs.

11. Be active. Post regularly. Use social media to keep top of mind in your industry, in the eyes of potential clients as well as in search engines.

12. Share unique content. People are more likely to engage with fresh content.

13. Create valuable content. If your content sucks and no one wants to engage or read it, then SEO will not help you.

A properly search engine optimized social media strategy can increase subscribers, fans, friends and followers just by using search engines.

Action:
List 10 keywords you can use based on keyword research.

Make Your Blog Shareable

As part of your social media strategy your blog editorial content calendar includes which social media platforms you plan to share the post on, when you will share and how often.

I recommend sharing on the date you publish, a week later and a month later. It's good to also create a plan on how you will share old blog posts.

Search engines love blogs; unique and frequent content is a great way to get ranked in search engines. Plan each post to promote your opt-ins and products and services. Mix in regular blog posts with evergreen blog posts (long, unique, and informative) and controversial blog posts (make a stand and say what's on your mind).

Make Your Blog Shareable

- Search Engine Optimize (SEO) all posts
- Branded image with each post
- Call to action with each post
- Embed Facebook updates in posts
- Embed Pinterest boards or images updates in posts
- Embed Instagram images updates in posts
- Use click to tweet in posts

Monitor and track your website using analytic tools such as Google Analytics. Measure how much traffic you get from each social media platform to your blog. Go a step further and track conversions.

> **Action:**
> **Optimize your blog for social media.**

Email

Use valuable content to get people to your website and reel them in with an awesome opt-in offer. Ensure your opt-in offer is not crap. If you're offering a gift, it should have a real value of at least $100. Don't offer crap - it's the quickest way to get people to unsubscribe.

Awesome Gift
- EBook
- Checklist
- Event (Teleseminar, Webinar or Live Event, Video or Audio Class)
- Video - tips and tricks and tutorials
- Audio - exclusive interview
- Quiz or Survey
- Promotional offer for product or service

Having a newsletter not only helps you build relationships it keeps you top of mind and is a great promotional tool.
- Turns leads to sales
- Builds your Awesome Nation
- Show you as an expert
- Great for branding
- Drives traffic to your website and social media platforms

Use social media in conjunction with your newsletter to start conversations. Get people to comment on your preferred social media platform by asking for feedback in your newsletter.

> **Action:**
> **Get people from your newsletter interacting on your**
> **social media.**

Offline

Social media is not your only form of marketing. In conjunction with other areas of online marketing such as blogging you should continue marketing offline.

Social media is a great way to meet new people, make new connections and find new clients.

Use offline opportunities to build connections.
Meet face to face with people you meet online. To deepen connections grab a coffee with someone you met online. If travelling let people know you will be in their neck of the woods and set up a meeting.

Take online offline by meeting and connecting with people. Watch online for local events to attend. Support your Awesome Nation by attending their events, shopping with them and promoting them.

To close the sale, you may have to meet face-to-face. Not everyone you meet online is comfortable doing business online. It may take a phone call, Skype chat or actual a face-to-face meeting to close the sale.

How does your social media support your offline promotions?
If you are attending or hosting an event, seminar, training, etc. post about it. Let people know before, post pics during and let people know how it was after.

Attend Meetups in your area. Find Meetups that your target audience belong to and start networking. Also, look for opportunities to be a guest speaker. Start your own Meetup.

If you have in-store promotions, let people know to come in and take advantage. On a slow day send out a message to come in with an impromptu promotion.

Show behind the scenes. What you're working on. What your desk looks like. Shipment day.

When I meet face-to-face with clients, I post it on social media with a picture of the both of us or their business card and tag them in the post.

Post pictures of new marketing material such as flyers, post cards, etc. even better start engagement by asking your Awesome Nation to choose which one they like better.

How does your offline promotions support social media?

If you are on television or radio, let people know how to find you on social media.

Offer people bonuses, or enter them into contests to connect with you on social media.

If you're advertising offline, include the social media logo to let people know to find you on social media.

- Promote your social media accounts offline:
- Email signature
- Phone message
- Print Materials such as
- Business card

- Flyers
- Postcards
- Trade Show Banners
- Thank you cards
- Appointment cards
- Brochures
- Presentation Folders
- Letterhead
- Envelopes
- Invoices

> **Action:**
> **Write down 3 people you would like to meet offline.**
> **Write down 3 ways social media can support your offline marketing.**
> **Write down 3 offline promotions to support social media.**

Chapter Seven
Check In

Metrics

Social Media can be a lot of static, and your marketing can get lost in the shuffle. How do you know if you are successful? Besides seeing actual sales - money in hand, you can track and monitor your social media success.

On a weekly and/or monthly basis review your online metrics. Use Google Analytics in conjunction with Bitly, Buffer, Hootsuite or other reporting tools and the social media platform analytics to track and monitor your success.

Learn more about your return on investment (ROI – time and money) as well as which posts brings the most traffic, engagement, and conversion.

Always track the results of your social media posts. Once you know what type of content your audience interacts with on social media, you can plan the type of information you are sharing as well as carefully create specific calls to action to increase results and sales.

Tracking is crucial, especially when running social media campaigns. When running campaigns, you always want to set up a special sales page or opt-in page to track results. You want to keep track of where people are coming from and what messages are resonating and making people take action. You want to carefully measure the results from individual campaigns to determine how they are performing. With this information, you can test and tweak your campaigns for maximum effectiveness.

Review your weekly, monthly and yearly stats to learn how to improve your social media strategy.

- Which day and time is better to post?
- Which hashtags are bringing in the most engagement?
- How many people are engaging - shares, likes, comments, etc. with your social media posts.
- Which posts, images, and videos have the most engagement and bring the most traffic to your website?
- How many people visit your website from social media and are they engaging on your website. Learn which blog posts do well on social media.
- Finally, how many people are converting from your social media posts. How many leads are you generating? How many sales are you making?

By reviewing your social media stats you can see if you are spending your time in the right place.

If you are not analyzing the results from your social media marketing, you are wasting your time on social media. How will you know if you're actions are making an impact? How will you know if it's working?

> **Action:**
> **Download and complete the Social Media Success Tracker, which includes Blog Stats, Monthly Success Tracker, and The Monthly And Yearly Social Media Stats.**

Social Media Mistakes

Don't Compare Your Behind-The-Scenes with Everyone Else's Highlight Reel - Steven Furtick

Here is a big list of do's and don'ts on social media.

1. Always follow the rules and regulations for each social media platform. If you don't, you can get your account suspended.
2. Do create a social media marketing plan, but adjust your specific tactics as you go. Be flexible and take the time to find out what works and what doesn't work.
3. Do commit the time and effort to maintain your social media marketing plan.
4. Do commit to at least 30 days if you are trying a new social media platform or new tactics.
5. Do pay attention to social media ethics.
6. Do show your passion; if you're not feeling it, don't post it.
7. Do write the way you speak.
8. Do listen to your clients through your social media and respond where appropriate
9. Do participate – Join the conversation.
10. Do pay attention to the metrics and analytics of your campaign.
11. Do pay attention to trends. Be prepared to change your campaign to match the most recent trends.
12. Do prepare to deal with how online users change, alter or use your brand's message. Have a plan for both good and bad customer feedback.

13. If you are sharing others content and can't answer what's in it for me of your preferred client, don't post it.
14. Do support promotional campaigns of your fans.
15. Do support the promotional campaigns of other non-competitive businesses on your social media sites in exchange for their support
16. Don't let perfect stop you from posting.
17. Don't let grammar stop you; your grammar does not have to be perfect.
18. Don't forget to add attribution when it's not your content.
19. Don't just post your own content
20. Don't post photos that will embarrass or humiliate someone or are unflattering
21. Don't share every moment of your day
22. Don't be disrespectful, offensive, vulgar or use language considered to be inflammatory
23. Don't be rude or difficult to deal with when engaging with your fans
24. Don't lie to your clients or hide the fact that you are advertising to them. Always be transparent with your intentions
25. Don't overdo it when promoting your business. You want to use social media to build relationships, notto overwhelm with ads.
26. Don't spam!

Do get into the daily habit of engagement. To build momentum and see results it's best to create daily habits with social media. I have developed 10-day social media challenges to

jumpstart the daily habit of using social media. It may seem hard to be on the big 5 social media platforms daily but that's why I developed social media engagement in 15 minutes a day. It allows you to schedule posts then take 5-15 minutes to engage every single day.

Action:
Follow these guidelines to social media success.

THANK-YOU
HOPE YOU ENJOYED READING
SOCIAL MEDIA MARKETING
HOW TO MASTER ENGAGEMENT IN 15 MINUTES A DAY

GET YOUR FREE SOCIAL MEDIA BONUSES!
http://bit.ly/social-bonus

PLEASE LEAVE A REVIEW ON AMAZON

The exercises in this book can be found in the **Social Media Marketing Workbook** and the **Social Media Marketing Planner**.

BE SURE TO GRAB YOUR COPIES
- Facebook Media Marketing Workbook -
- Google+ Workbook and Planner -
- LinkedIn Workbook and Planner -
- Twitter Workbook and Planner -
- Pinterest Workbook and Planner -
- Instagram Workbook and Planner -

ALSO LOOK OUT FOR
Authentic Marketing – The Three E's of Online Marketing: Ethical, Effortless, Engaging

Connect with Dwainia Grey on LinkedIn, Google+, Facebook, Twitter, Pinterest and Instagram
dwainiagrey.me

BONUS

Join the **Empowerpreneur League** Facebook Group
to network with others for support, feedback,
brainstorming, growth and tips. This group is 100% Free
and made up of Empowerpreneurs across the world.
http://bit.ly/empowerpreneur-league

You can also join us on LinkedIn.
http://bit.ly/empowerpreneur-marketing

BE SURE TO GRAB YOUR COPIES
- **Facebook Workbook and Planner** -
- **Google+ Workbook and Planner** -
- **LinkedIn Workbook and Planner** -
- **Twitter Workbook and Planner** -
- **Pinterest Workbook and Planner** -
- **Instagram Workbook and Planner** -

www.ingramcontent.com/pod-product-compliance
Lightning Source LLC
Chambersburg PA
CBHW060947050326
40689CB00012B/2577